Contents

Walking Tour Map .... pg. 2

Audio Track List .... pg. 4

Stop 1: Visitor Center .... pg. 6

Stop 2: The Sunken Road .... pg. 12

Stop 3: Cobb Memorial .... pg. 14

Stop 4: Innis House .... pg. 15

Stop 5: Stratton House .... pg. 18

Stop 6: The Canal Ditch .... pg. 22

Stop 7: The Stone Wall .... pg. 26

Stop 8: Marye's Heights .... pg. 29

Stop 9: National Cemetery .... pg. 33

Bibliography .... pg. 39

Acknowledgments .... pg. 43

Quiz Answers .... pg. 43

Credits .... pg. 44

Walking Tour Map

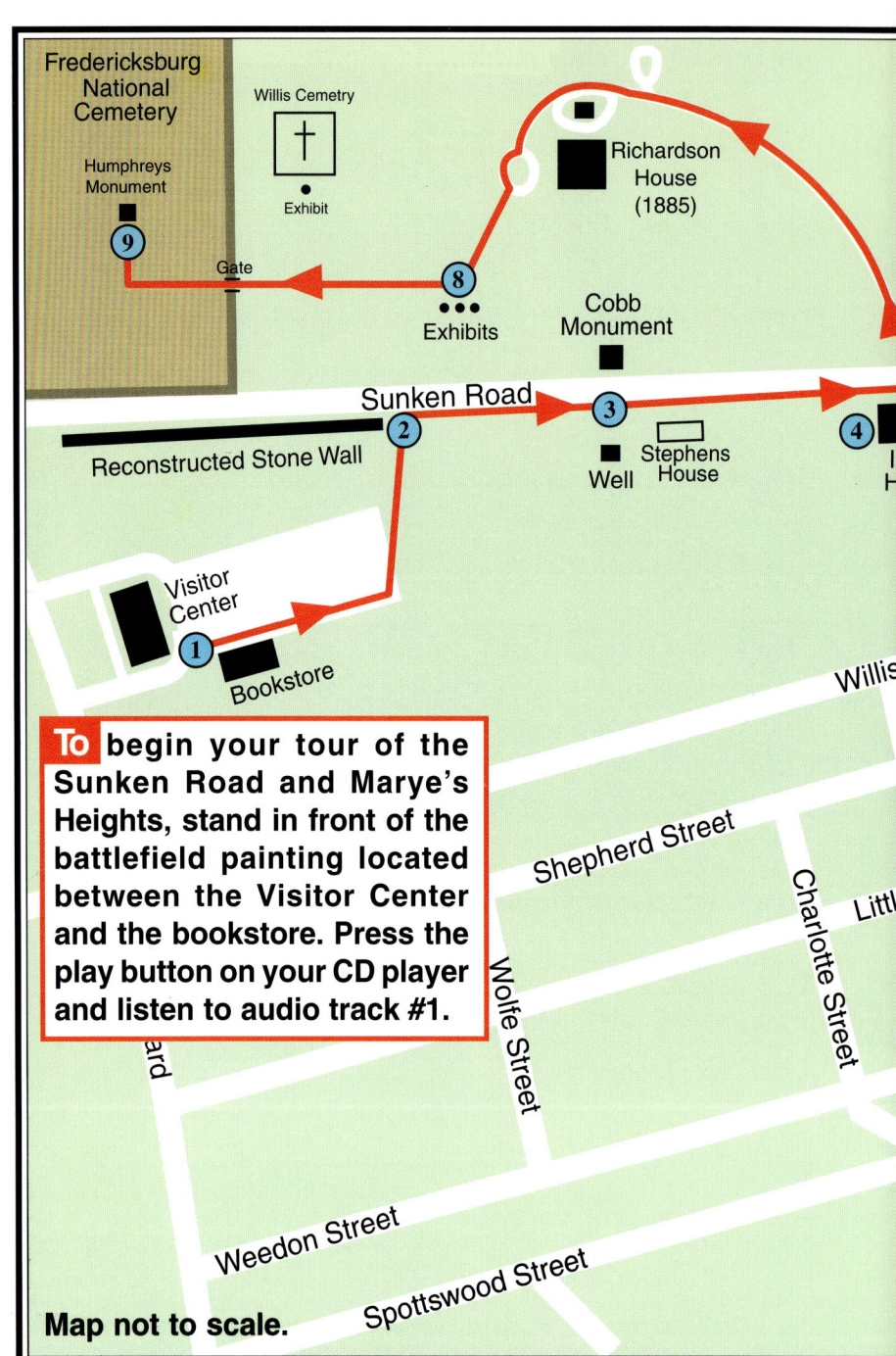

Map not to scale.

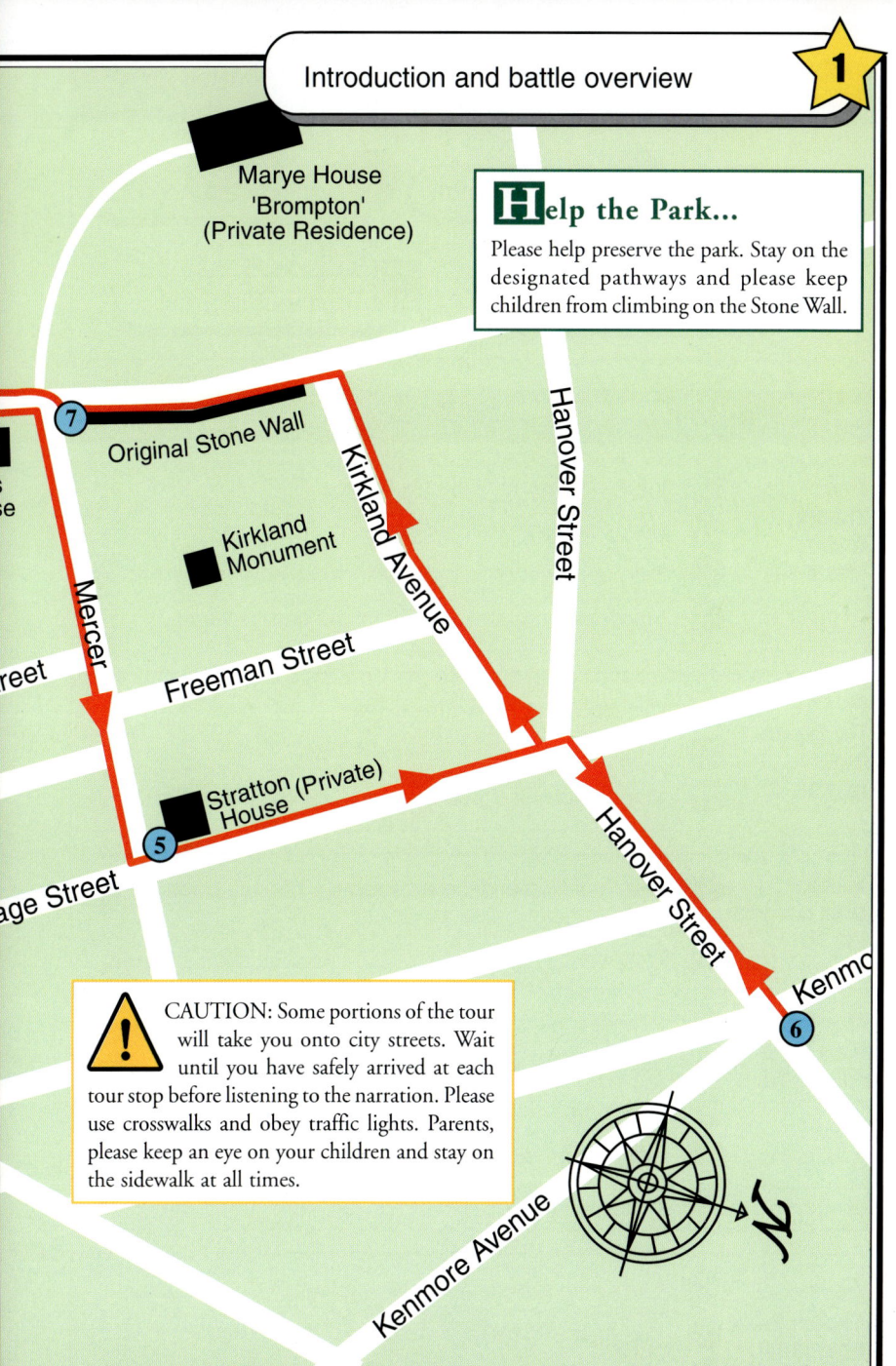

Walking Tour Map

Audio Key

- ⭐ # History
- 🔵 # Union Account
- 🔴 # Confederate Account
- 🟢 # Civilian Account
- 🟨 # Topics of Interest

Tour Stop	Track #	Audio Description
Stop 1: Visitors Center (pgs. 6-11)	1 ⭐	Introduction and battle overview
	2 ⭐	Historical context of the battle
	3 🔴	Pontoon bridges come under fire from Confederate sharpshooters
	4 🟢	Fredericksburg civilian remembers fleeing the city
Stop 2: The Sunken Road (pgs. 12-13)	5 ⭐	Description of the Sunken Road
	6 🟢	Union soldiers loot Fredericksburg
	7 🟨	The creation of Fredericksburg & Spotsylvania NMP
Stop 3: Cobb Memorial (pg. 14)	8 🔴	Profile of Confederate commander Thomas Cobb
Stop 4: Innis House (pgs. 15-17)	9 ⭐	Overview of Union attacks against the Sunken Road
	10 🟨	The Innis House
	11 🔵	A Union soldier recalls preparing to go into combat
	12 🔵	Profile of Union officer Col. Henry I. Zinn
	13 🔴	A Confederate perspective of the first wave of attacks
Stop 5: Stratton House (pgs. 18-21)	14 ⭐	The swale that saved the lives of many Union soldiers
	15 🔵	The Irish Brigade advances
	16 🔵	Profile of Union Col. Edward E. Cross

Walking Tour Map

Tour Stop	Track #	Audio Description
Stop 6: The Canal Ditch (pgs. 22-25)	17	The canal ditch and continued Union attacks
	18	A Union soldier recalls the terrifying effect of artillery
	19	Union Corps commander Darius Couch recalls the terrible losses sustained by his men
Stop 7: The Stone Wall (pgs. 26-28)	20	The original stone wall
	21	A Confederate soldier recalls the futility of the Union attacks
	22	The statue of Richard Kirkland, the Angel of Marye's Heights
Stop 8: Marye's Heights (pgs. 29-33)	23	Burnside calls for more attacks against the Sunken Road
	24	A Confederate soldier recalls the devastation in front of the stone wall
	25	A family torn apart by war: the story of Confederate Brig. Gen. John Rogers Cooke
	26	A description of artillery projectiles
Stop 9: National Cemetery (pgs. 24-39)	27	The final assaults against the Sunken Road
	28	A Union soldier remembers the heart-rending aftermath of battle
	29	A Confederate soldier inspects the fields in front of the Sunken Road following the battle
	30	A Fredericksburg resident returns home
	31	The origins of Fredericksburg's National Cemetery
	32	Epilogue: The aftermath of Fredericksburg

Portable CD Player Controls

Skip Back	Play/Pause	Skip Forward

South of Fredericksburg, William Franklin's Left Grand Division was ordered to attack the right end of the Confederate line. Once Franklin's attack had begun, Sumner's Right Grand Division would attack the Confederate line on Marye's Heights.

Visitor Center

Army of the Potomac
Federal
118,000 men
360 Cannon

Burnside
Commander

Left Grand Division	Center Grand Division	Right Grand Division

Franklin	Hooker	Sumner
I Corps	III Corps	II Corps
	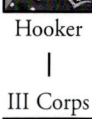	
Reynolds	Stoneman	Couch
VI Corps	V Corps	IX Corps

Smith	Butterfield	Willcox

Army Organization

 **Army** (XXXX)

 **Corps** (XXX)

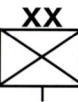 **Division** (XX)

 Brigade (X)

 Regiment (III)

These symbols are used on the battlefield maps in this book to denote the general locations of troops.

Army of Northern Virginia
Confederate
78,000 men
279 Cannon

Lee
Commander

First Corps	Second Corps

Longstreet	Jackson

Note: Confederate corps were usually named after their commanders.

TravelBrains Trivia Questions 1

Approximately how large was the entire United States Army just prior to the Civil War?

A. 6,000 men

B. 14,000 men

C. 58,000 men

(Quiz answers are located on page 43)

Visitor Center

2 Historical context of the Battle of Fredericksburg.

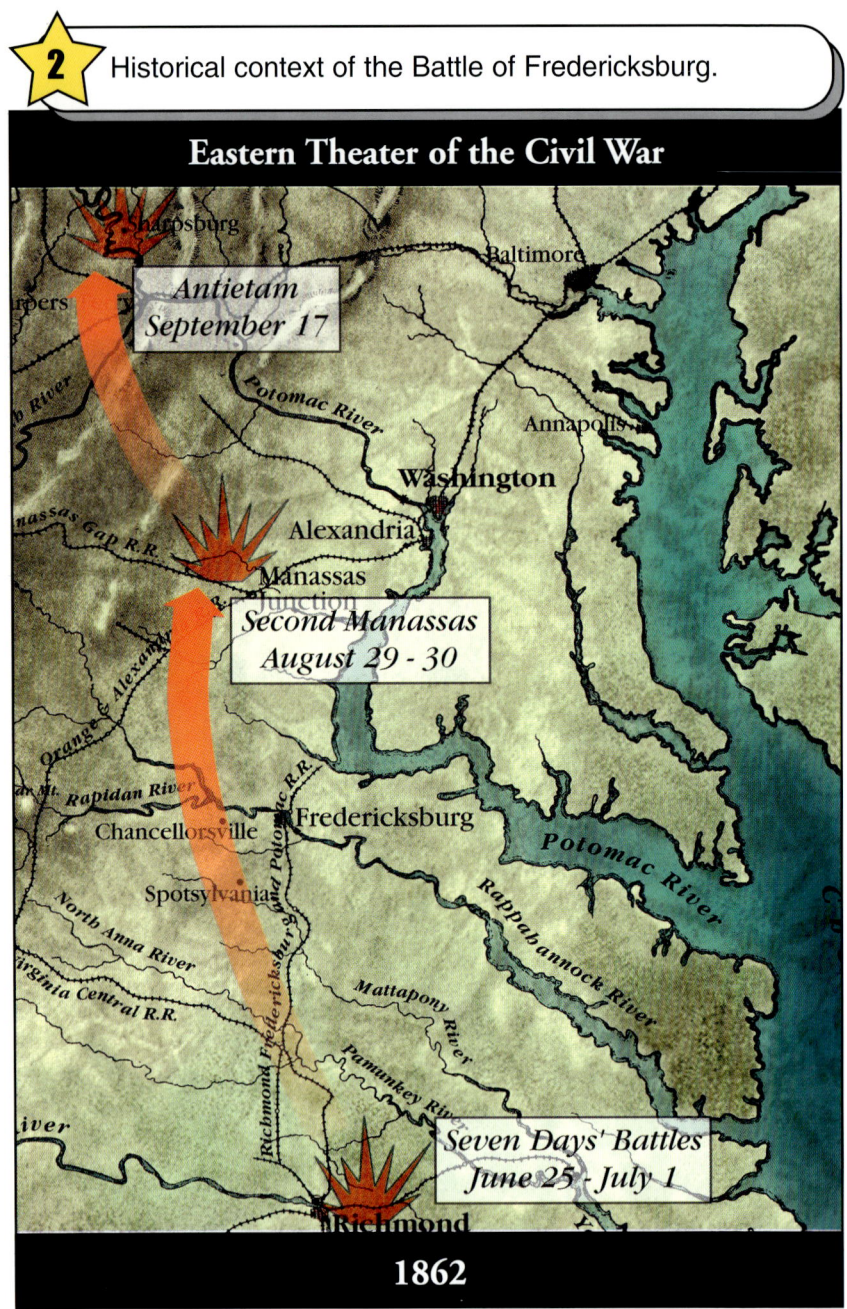

After taking command of the Army of Northern Virginia, Robert E. Lee drove the Union army away from the gates of Richmond during the Seven Days' Battles. Next, Lee crushed Union General John Pope's Army of Virginia during the Second Manassas campaign and then launched an invasion of the North. Following the Battle of Antietam, Lee was forced to retreat back to Virginia.

Visitor Center

Robert E. Lee

George B. McClellan

Abraham Lincoln

Ambrose E. Burnside

Visitor Center

2

A ponton used to construct floating bridges during the Civil War.

A sketch of Union engineers assembling a Pontoon Bridge at Fredericksburg, December 11, 1862.

3 Pontoon bridges come under fire from Confederate sharpshooters

For some seven hours, Southern marksmen of William Barksdale's brigade prevented Union engineers from completing the pontoon bridge.

4 A Fredericksburg civilian remembers fleeing the city

Frustrated by the Confederate sharpshooters, Burnside ordered 150 cannons to open fire on the city. The fire storm of shot and shell was spectacular, but it failed to drive Barksdale's men from their hiding spots.

The Sunken Road

5. History of the Sunken Road

A photograph looking west towards Marye's Heights and the Sunken Road.

6. Description of looting by Union soldiers

A sketch of Union soldiers looting in the streets of Fredericksburg.

7 The creation of Fredericksburg and Spotsylvania National Military Park.

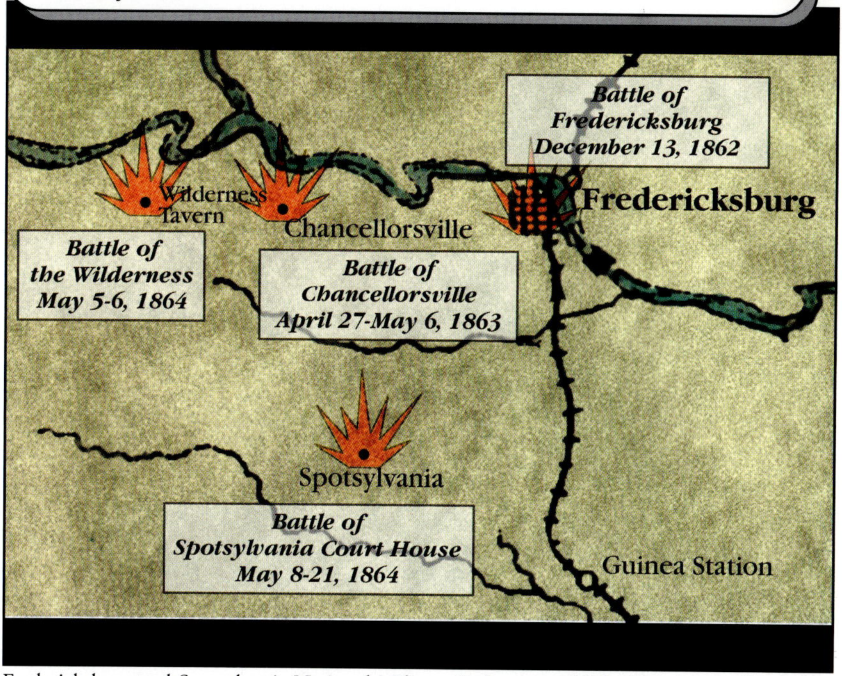

Battle of Fredericksburg December 13, 1862
Fredericksburg
Wilderness Tavern
Chancellorsville
Battle of the Wilderness May 5-6, 1864
Battle of Chancellorsville April 27-May 6, 1863
Spotsylvania
Battle of Spotsylvania Court House May 8-21, 1864
Guinea Station

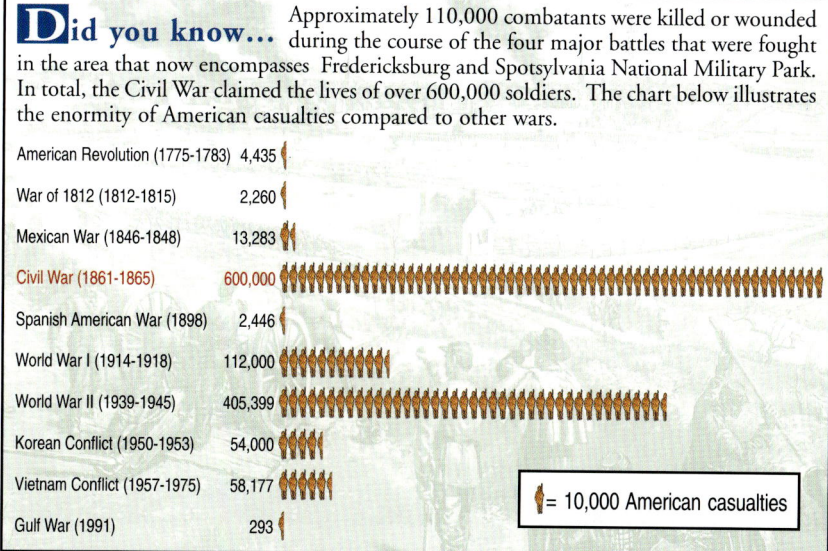

Fredericksburg and Spotsylvania National Military Park was established by an act of Congress in 1927. The park includes the battlefields of Fredericksburg, Chancellorsville, Wilderness, and Spotsylvania.

Did you know... Approximately 110,000 combatants were killed or wounded during the course of the four major battles that were fought in the area that now encompasses Fredericksburg and Spotsylvania National Military Park. In total, the Civil War claimed the lives of over 600,000 soldiers. The chart below illustrates the enormity of American casualties compared to other wars.

American Revolution (1775-1783) 4,435
War of 1812 (1812-1815) 2,260
Mexican War (1846-1848) 13,283
Civil War (1861-1865) 600,000
Spanish American War (1898) 2,446
World War I (1914-1918) 112,000
World War II (1939-1945) 405,399
Korean Conflict (1950-1953) 54,000
Vietnam Conflict (1957-1975) 58,177
Gulf War (1991) 293
= 10,000 American casualties

Cobb Memorial

8 Profile of Confederate commander Thomas R. R. Cobb

Thomas R. R. Cobb

Innis House

Overview of first wave of Union attacks

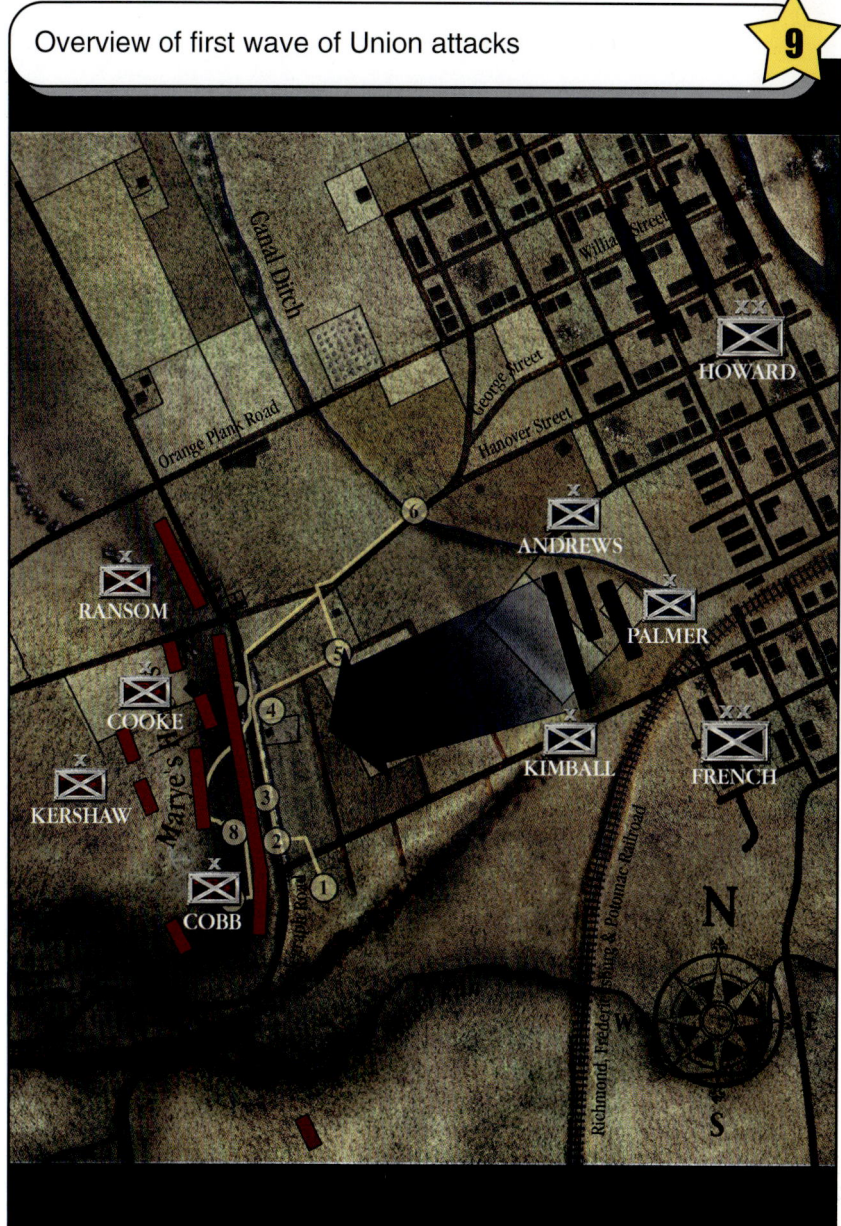

At approximately noon, Union Brigadier General William H. French advanced his division against the Sunken Road. His three brigades moved forward across the open terrain lined up one after the other.

Note: The maps depicted in this guidebook show the terrain and buildings as they appeared at the time of the battle.

Innis House

10 The Innis House

A photograph of the Innis House and Sunken Road taken during the 1800s.

One for the kids...
If you look through the window into the house, you can see numerous holes in the walls. These holes are the result of the heavy rifle and cannon fire that raged around the Innis House on December 13, 1862.

11 Union soldier Benjamin Borton describes the scene as Kimball's Brigade prepares to attack the Sunken Road

Brig. Gen. Nathan Kimball

TravelBrains Trivia Questions 2

Which Confederate General was known as Lee's "Old War Horse"?

A. James Longstreet
B. Stonewall Jackson
C. J.E.B. Stuart

Did you know...
Surgeons used a bone saw similar to this one to amputate the limbs of soldiers.

Innis House

> **12** A profile of Union officer Henry Zinn

The battle flag of the 130th Pennsylvania Volunteer Infantry Regiment.

Col. Henry I. Zinn

Sword of Col. Henry I. Zinn

> **13** Confederate artillerist William M. Owen describes the first wave of Union attacks

Did you know...

The Minié Ball was named after French army officer Claude-Etienne Minié. Upon firing, the hollow base of the bullet would expand in the barrel forcing it against the rifle grooves that lined the tube. As a result, the bullet would spiral out of the barrel and achieve greater accuracy and range.

1st Lt. William M. Owen

17

Stratton House

14 The swale that saved the lives of many Union soldiers

The Stratton House can be seen in this painting of the Fredericksburg battlefield. It is the house with

Stratton House

the double chimney on the left side of the painting.

Stratton House

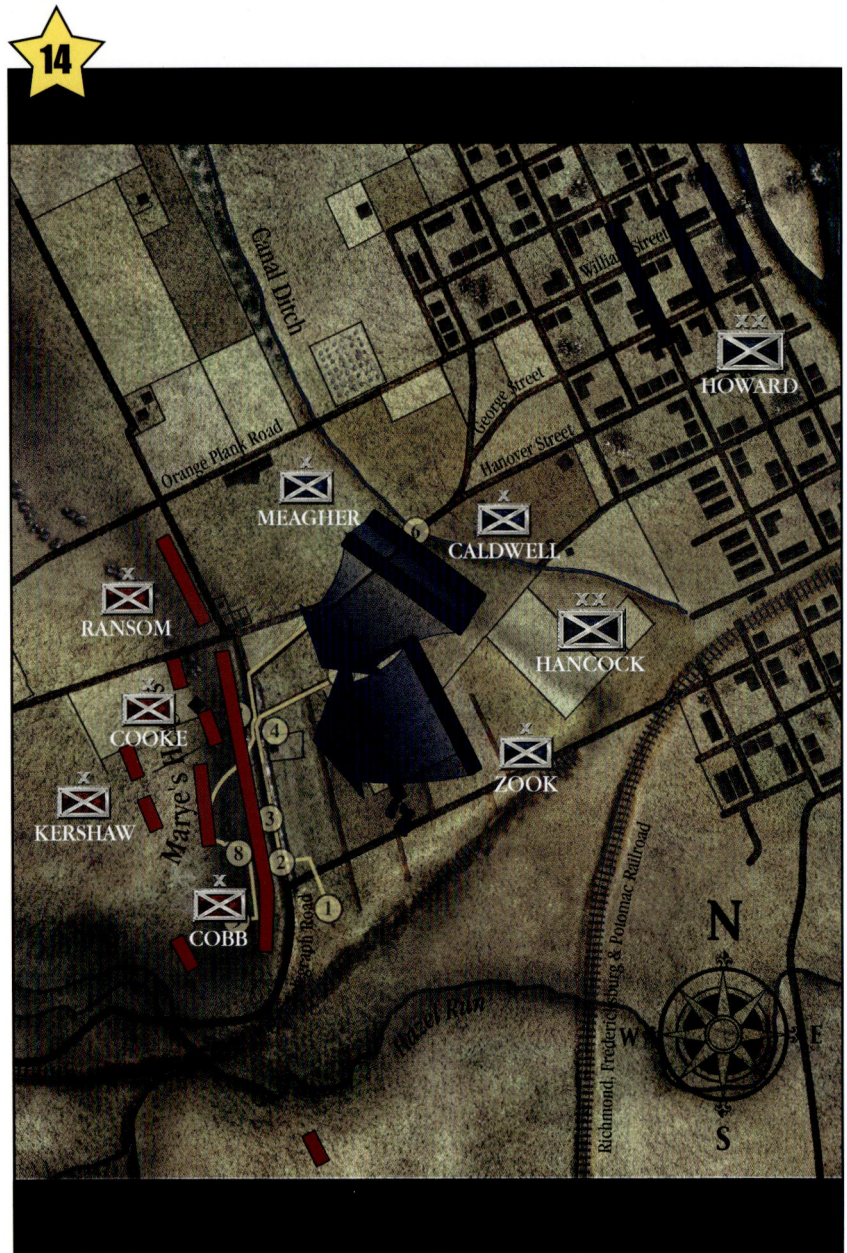

After French's attack stalled, General Hancock advanced his three brigades. Despite their best efforts, his men could not reach the stone wall. Within the span of roughly an hour, two Federal divisions had been devastated. Hancock and French began sending urgent pleas for reinforcements.

Stratton House

15 The Irish Brigade advances

In addition to the American flag, Irish Brigade regiments usually carried a green flag like the one illustrated above into battle.

Brig. Gen. Thomas F. Meagher

16 Profile of Union Col. Edward E. Cross

Did you know...

Despite surviving the slaughter of Antietam's Bloody Lane and Fredericksburg's Marye's Heights, Cross had a strong premonition that the fighting at Gettysburg would be his last. On the second day of battle at Gettysburg, Cross prepared to lead his brigade into the Wheatfield. Usually he asked his orderly to tie a red bandana around his head prior to battle. But on this day, he requested a black bandana which was duly noted by the Colonel's aid. During the fighting in the Wheatfield, Cross was shot in the stomach and died shortly thereafter.

Col. Edward E. Cross

The Canal Ditch

17 The Canal Ditch and continued Union attacks

This 1864 photograph of the Fredericksburg battlefield reveals the open terrain that Federal soldiers

This sketch by the famous Civil War artist Alfred Waud depicts the fighting on December 13 from his

The Canal Ditch

had to cross to make it to the Sunken Road.

viewpoint atop a church steeple in Fredericksburg.

The Canal Ditch

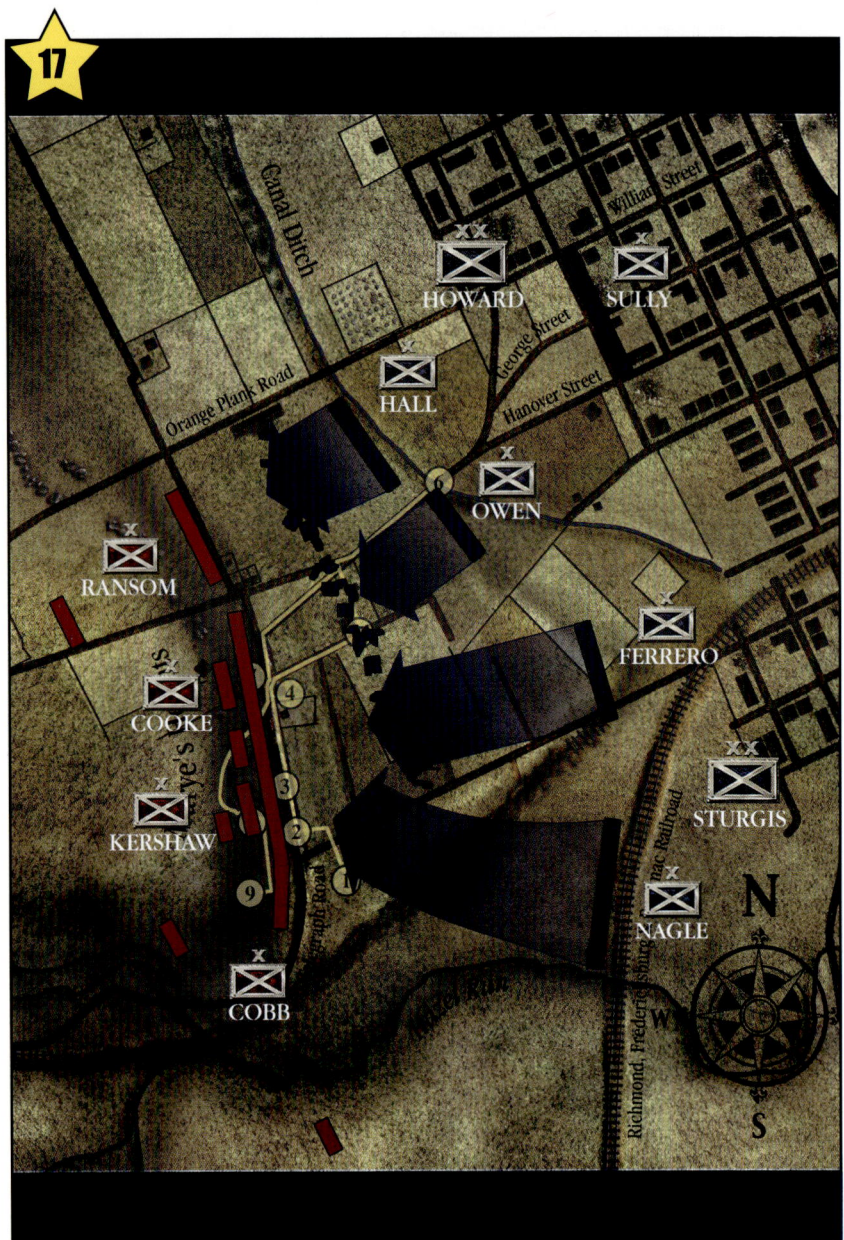

By 1:00 PM Union General Oliver O. Howard advanced two brigades across the canal ditch to support the embattled troops of French and Hancock. But like the previous two efforts, Howard's men were soon mired in front of the Confederate defenses exchanging fire as best they could. Believing that Confederate troops moving to reinforce the Confederate line were massing for a counterattack, Union Brigadier General Samuel D. Sturgis ordered his two brigades to shore up the Union left flank.

The Canal Ditch

> **18** A Union soldier in Sully's Brigade recalls the terrifying effect of Confederate artillery

Did you know…

Albert James Myer, the father of the US Army Signal Corps, started his military career as an Army Doctor. While serving as a medical officer in Texas in 1856, Myer invented a visual system of communication called "wigwag." "Wigwag" used flags in the daytime and torches at night. Myer was the first Signal Officer when the Signal Corps was formed on June 21, 1860. At Fredericksburg, Myer's Signal Corps ran a telegraph line to Franklin's Grand Division Headquarters and also Sumner's Headquarters at Chatham. Because dense smoke prevented observation of Franklin's progress on the left end of the battlefield, the telegraph played an important role in giving Burnside an idea on how the battle was developing.

Brig. Gen. Alfred Sully

> **19** Union Corpse commander Darius Couch recalls the terrible losses sustained by his men

A Civil War Telegraph Key

Did you know…

Fredericksburg was the boyhood home of George Washington. According to legend, it was here that the future first President chopped down the cherry tree and threw the silver dollar across the river.

Maj. Gen. Darius N. Couch

The Stone Wall

20 Description of the original stone wall

By late afternoon, the Confederates were standing several rows deep behind the stone wall.

The Stone Wall

The Stone Wall

21 A Confederate soldier recalls the futility of the Union attacks

Pvt. Alexander Hunter

TravelBrains Trivia Questions 3

Out of 34 states at the beggining of the Civil War, how many offically left the Union to join the Confederacy?

A. 9
B. 10
C. 11

Did you know...

Hardtack was a staple of the Civil War soldier's diet. A hard biscuit made of flour and water, it was ideal for military use because it was inexpensive, easy to transport and did not decay or spoil quickly.

22 The statue of Richard R. Kirkland, the Angel of Marye's Heights

Sgt. Richard R. Kirkland

Brig. Gen. Joseph B. Kershaw

Marye's Heights

Burnside calls for more attacks against the Sunken Road

A sketch of the Washington Artillery on Marye's Heights.

Maj. Gen. Joseph Hooker

Brig. Gen. Andrew A. Humphreys

Marye's Heights

A post-battle photograph of Brompton, the Marye family estate. Note the bullet pock-marked walls.

 A Confederate soldier recalls the devastation in front of the stone wall

Lt. Charles S. Powell

Did you know...

Hot air balloons were used for reconnaissance during the Civil War. During the Battle of Fredericksburg Lt. Col. William W. Teall ascended several times into the air using the hot air balloon "Eagle." Viewing the battlefield at an altitude of 800 to 900 feet, Lt. Col. Teall later wrote "...The scene from this height and at this moment of the battle was magnificent beyond description."

Marye's Heights

A family torn apart by war: the story of Confederate commander John Rogers Cooke

Brig. Gen. John R. Cooke

Brig. Gen. Philip St. George Cooke

D id you know...

In 1859, J.E.B. Stuart was serving temporarily as the aid to Lt. Col. Robert E. Lee in the 2nd US Cavalry. When abolitionist John Brown seized the Harpers Ferry arsenal that year, Lee was ordered to arrest him. Under a white flag, Stuart approached Brown's temporary fort to speak with the leader of the revolt. To his amazement, Stuart recognized Brown from his service in Kansas in the 1850s. There Brown had made a name for himself as a man unafraid to shed blood in the name of the anti-slavery movement.

Maj. Gen. J.E.B. Stuart

 TravelBrains
Trivia Questions 4

What was the population of Fredericksburg in 1860?

A. 5,000
B. 10,000
C. 60,000

Marye's Heights

26 — A description of Civil War artillery projectiles

Solid Shot

Solid Shot was a round ball or elongated projectile made of solid iron. It was typically used at longer ranges against massed troops, fortifications, and enemy batteries. Solid shot (or bolts as they were sometimes called when fired from rifled cannons) were not designed to explode.

Shell

A shell was a cast iron projectile (round or elongated) filled with black powder. A fuse that was ignited by the discharge of the cannon caused the shell to explode, sending twisted pieces of iron raining down on a target. An experienced artilleryman was capable of accurately timing the fuse to explode the shell over his target.

Canister

Canister was a tin can filled with iron balls (a little smaller than the size of golf balls) packed in sawdust. This type of ammunition effectively turned the cannon into a large shotgun. It was used at close range against infantry. In extreme cases, double and triple canister rounds were packed into the cannon muzzle and fired.

Case Shot

Case shot, sometimes called shrapnel, was a hollow iron shell (round or elongated) filled with round balls and sealed in melted rosin or sulphur. A powder charge in the core of the shell was ignited by a timed fuse. When the shell exploded the balls and twisted fragments of iron tore through soldiers and horses.

12-Pounder Napoleon

This famous cannon was named after Emperor Napoleon III of France. The term "12-Pounder" comes from the twelve-pound artillery round it fired. By the end of the Civil War it was by far the most widely used artillery piece in both armies. It had an effective range of one mile and could fire solid shot, shell, case shot and canister rounds. Made of bronze, the tube alone weighed over 1,200 pounds.

National Cemetery

The final assaults against the Sunken Road — 27

At 3:00 PM, Union Brigadier General Charles Griffin received instructions to help General Sturgis' command. He moved forward with 6,000 men in three brigades. At approximately 4:00 P.M. Union Division commander Andrew Humphreys launched his two brigades at the stone wall but was unable to pierce the enemy defenses.

National Cemetery

28 A Union soldier remembers the heart rending aftermath of battle

Burial of dead soldiers following the battle of Second Fredericksburg.

29 A Confederate soldier inspects the fields in front of the stone wall following the battle

A sketch of Union soldiers being buried following the battle.

National Cemetery

30   A Fredericksburg resident returns home

A painting of Fredericksburg residents returning to their home after the battle.

31   The origins of the Fredericksburg National Cemetery

Did you know...

Ambrose Burnside left the military service in 1853 to start a firearms company. After his first company burnt down, Burnside formed the Bristol Firearm Company in January 1854. Financed by his wife's wealthy family, Burnside pursued the production of a carbine that implemented several innovative features that made the weapon more reliable. In all, five different models of the Burnside carbine were produced.

National Cemetery

32 — Epilogue: The aftermath of Fredericksburg

Gen. Robert E. Lee

National Cemetery

32

Abraham Lincoln

National Cemetery

32

Maj. Gen. Ambrose E. Burnside

BIBLIOGRAPHY

Many sources were consulted during the completion of this work. Both manuscript and printed sources were utilized from the Fredericksburg and Spotsylvania National Military Park as well as the United States Army Military History Institute located at Carlisle Barracks, Pennsylvania. The National Archives in Washington, DC also provided valuable documentation in the completion of the project.

Archival and Manuscript Sources

Harvard University Archives, Cambridge, MA:

>   Henry L. Abbott Biographical Material.

>   Lane W. Brandon Biographical Material.

National Archives Records Administration, Washington, DC.

>   Record Group 15. Civil War Pension Records.

>   Record Group 94. Compiled Military Service Records of Union Soldiers.

>   Record Group 109. Compiled Military Service Records of Confederate Soldiers.

Fredericksburg and Spotsylvania National Military Park, Fredericksburg, VA.

>   Bound Manuscript Volumes.

Published Sources

Adams, John G.B. *Reminiscences of the Nineteenth Massachusetts Regiment.* Boston, MA: Wright & Potter, 1899.

Bliss, Zenas. "Types and Traditions of the Old Army: Extracts from the Unpublished Memoirs of Major General Zenas R. Bliss, U. S. A." *Journal of the Military Service Institution.* Volume 38. (May-June 1906).

Boatner, Mark M., III. *The Civil War Dictionary.* New York, NY: David McKay Company, 1959.

Borton, Benjamin. *On the Parallels or Chapters of Inner History A Story of the Rappahannock.* Woodstown, NJ: Monitor-Register Print, 1903.

Bruce, George A. *The Twentieth Regiment of Massachusetts Volunteer Infantry 1861-1865.* Boston and New York: Houghton, Mifflin and Company, 1906.

Carroll, Les. *The Angel of Marye's Heights: Sergeant Richard Kirkland's Extraordinary Deed at Fredericksburg.* Columbia, SC: Palmetto Books, 1994.

Child, William A. *A History of the Fifth Regiment, New Hampshire Volunteers in the American Civil War.* Bristol, NH: R. W. Musgrove, Printer, 1893.

Coats, Earl J. and Dean S. Thomas. *An Introduction to Civil War Small Arms.* Gettysburg, PA: Thomas Publications, 1990.

Coggins, Jack. *Arms and Equipment of the Civil War.* Garden City, NY: Doubleday and Company, 1962; reprint, Wilmington, NC: Broadfoot Publishing, 1990.

Crute, Joseph H., Jr. *Units of the Confederate States Army.* Midlothian, VA: Derwent Books, 1987.

Daily Press (Newport News, VA) May 28 and 29, 1898.

Davis, William C. *The Confederate General.* Volumes 1-6. Harrisburg, PA: National Historical Society, 1991.

Ellis, William Arba comp and ed. *Norwich University 1819-1911 Her History, Her Graduates, Her Roll of Honor.* Volume 2. Montpelier, VT: The Capital City Press, 1911.

Faust, Patricia L., ed. *Historical Times Illustrated Encyclopedia of the Civil War.* New York, NY: Harper and Row Publishers, 1986.

Gallagher, Gary W., ed. *The Fredericksburg Campaign: Decision on the Rappahannock.* Chapel Hill, NC: University of North Carolina Press, 1995.

Galwey, Thomas F. *The Valiant Hours: Narrative of "Captain Brevet," An Irish-American in the Army of the Potomac.* Harrisburg, PA: Stackpole Books, 1961.

Gerry, H. E. *Campfire Entertainment and the True History of Robert Henry Hendershot The Drummer Boy of the Rappahannock.* Chicago, IL: Hack and Anderson, 1903.

Goolrick, William K. *Rebels Resurgent.* Time Life The Civil War Series. Alexandria, VA: Time-Life books, 1985.

Hagerty, Edward J. *Collis' Zouaves: The 114th Pennsylvania Volunteers in the Civil War.* Baton Rouge: Louisiana University Press, 1997.

Heitman, Francis B. *Historical Register and Dictionary of the United States Army: from its Organization, September 29, 1789 to March 2, 1903.* Volume 1 Washington: GPO, 1903; reprint, Gaithersburg, MD: Olde Soldiers Books, Inc. 1988.

Henderson, G.F.R. *The Campaign of Fredericksburg, Nov.-Dec., 1862: A Tactical Study For Officers.* London, England: Gale & Polden, 1891.

Higginson, Thomas W. ed. *Harvard Memorial Biographies. 2 Volumes.* Cambridge, MA: Sever and Francis, 1867.

Hopkins, William P. *The Seventh Regiment Rhode Island Volunteers in the Civil War, 1862-1865.* Providence, RI: Snow & Farnham Printers, 1903.

Harrison, Noel G. *Fredericksburg Civil War Sites*. 2 Volumes. Lynchburg, VA: H. E. Howard, Inc., 1995.

Hunt, Roger D. and Jack R. Brown. *Brevet Generals in Blue*. Gaithersburg, MD: Olde Soldiers Books, 1990.

Johnson, Robert U. and Clarence C. Buell, eds. *Battles and Leaders of the Civil War*. Volume 3. New York, NY: Century Company, 1886; reprint, Thomas Yoseloff, Inc., 1956.

Kepler, William. *History of the Three Months' and Three Years' Service From April 16th, 1861, to June 22d, 1864, of the Fourth Regiment Ohio Volunteer Infantry in the War For the Union*. Cleveland, Ohio: Leader Printing Company, 1886; reprint, Huntington, WV: Blue Acorn Press, 1886.

Krick, Robert K. *Lee's Colonels: A Biographical Register of Field Officers of the Army of Northern Virginia*. 4th Edition, Revised. Dayton, OH: Morningside Books, 1996.

Luvaas, Jay, and Nelson, Harold W. *The U.S. Army War College Guide to the Battles of Chancellorsville and Fredericksburg*. Carlisle, PA: South Mountain Press, 1988.

McWhintey, Grady and Perry D. Jamieson. *Attack and Die: Civil War Military Tactics and the Southern Heritage*. University, AL: University of Alabama Press, 1982.

Mathless, Paul. ed. *Fredericksburg*. Voices of the Civil War Series. Alexandria, VA: Time-Life Books, 1997.

Miller, Francis T. ed. *The Photographic History of the Civil War*. 10 Volumes. New York, NY, 1911; reprint, New York, NY: Thomas Yoseloff, 1957.

Miller, Richard F., & Mooney, Robert F. "Across the River and Into the Streets: The 20th Massachusetts Infantry and the Street Fight for Fredericksburg." *Civil War Regiments*. Volume 4. Number 4.

One hundred and Thirtieth Regiment Pennsylvania Volunteer Infantry Ceremonies and Addresses at the Dedication of the Monument at Bloody Lane, Antietam Battlefield September 17, 1904; Letters of Colonel H. I. Zinn Roster of Survivors. NP, 1904.

Palfrey, Francis W. *In Memoriam, H.L.A*. Boston, MA: Privately Printed, 1864.

O'Reilly, Frank A. "'Busted Up and Gone to Hell': The Assault of the Pennsylvania Reserves at Fredericksburg." *Civil War Regiments*. Volume 4. Number 4.

_____. "Stonewall" Jackson at Fredericksburg: The Battle of Prospect Hill, December 13, 1862. Lynchburg, VA: H. E. Howard, Inc., 1993.

_____. *Battle of Fredericksburg*. Map set of five maps. NP. 1997.

Robertson, James I., Jr. *Stonewall Jackson: the Man, the Soldier, the Legend*. New York, NY: MacMillan Publishing, 1997.

Robertson, John, comp. *Michigan in the War.* Lansing, MI: W. S. George and Company, 1880.

Sauers, Richard A. *Advance the Colors! Pennsylvania Civil War Battle Flags.* Harrisburg, PA: Capital Preservation Committee of the Commonwealth of Pennsylvania, 1991.

Sawyer, Franklin. *A Military History of the 8th Regiment Ohio Volunteer Infantry, Its Battles, Marches and Army Movements.* Cleveland, OH: Fairbanks and Company Printers, 1881.

Scott, Robert G., ed. *Fallen Leaves: The Civil War Letters of Major Henry Livermore Abbott.* Kent, OH: Kent State University Press, 1991.

Scott, Robert N. comp. *The War of the Rebellion: A Compilation of the Official Records of the Union and Confederate Armies.* Series I. Volume 21. Washington, DC: GPO, 1888.

Spangler, Edward W. *My Little War Experience with Historical Sketches and Memorabilia.* York, PA: York Daily Publishing Company, 1904.

Stackpole, Edward J. *Drama on the Rappahannock: The Fredericksburg Campaign.* Second Edition, Harrisburg, PA: Stackpole Books, 1991.

Starr, Stephen Z. *The Union Cavalry in the Civil War.* 3 Volumes. Baton Rouge, LA: Louisiana State University Press, 1979.

Thomas, Dean S. *Round Ball to Rim Fire A History of Civil War Small Arms Ammunition.* Part I. Gettysburg, PA: Thomas Publications, 1997.

_____. *Cannons An Introduction to Civil War Artillery.* Gettysburg, PA: Thomas Publications, 1985.

UDC. SC Div. John D. Kennedy Chapter. *Richard Kirkland, C.S.A.* Camden, SC: Walker, Evans & Cogswell, 1910.

Waitt, Ernest L. *History of the Nineteenth Regiment Massachusetts Volunteer Infantry, 1861-1865.* Salem, MA: Salem Press, 1906.

Warner, Ezra J. *Generals in Gray.* Baton Rouge, LA: Louisiana State University Press, 1959.

_____. *Generals in Blue.* Baton Rouge, LA: Louisiana State University Press, 1964.

Whan, Vorin W., Jr. *Fiasco at Fredericksburg.* Gaithersburg, MD: Butternut Press, 1986.

Wise, Jennings. *The Long Arm of Lee.* 2 Volumes. Lynchburg, VA: J. P. Bell Company, 1915; reprint, Lincoln, NE: University of Nebraska Press, 1991.

Acknowledgments

TravelBrains wishes to extend a special thanks to the staff at Fredericksburg & Spotsylvania National Military Park for all the support and feedback they have provided us in the development of the Fredericksburg Expedition Guide and Field Guide. We would also like to acknowledge the assistance and support of the following institutions and individuals during the course of this project:

Institutions and Collections

Anne S. K. Brown Collection, John Hay Library, Brown University
Capital Preservation Committee, Commonwealth of PA, Harrisburg, PA
Fields of Glory, Gettysburg, PA
Frank & Marie-Therese Wood Print Collections, Alexandria, VA
Fredericksburg & Spotsylvania National Military Park
Gallon Historical Art, Gettysburg, PA
Gregory A. Coco Collection
Harvard University Archives, Pusey Library, Cambridge, MA
Library of Congress, Washington, DC
Motts Military Museum, Groveport, OH
National Archives and Records Administration, Washington, DC
South Caroliniana Library, University of South Carolina, Columbia, SC
United States Army Military History Institute, Carlisle Barracks, PA
Virginia Military Institute, Lexington, VA

Individuals

John Adams	Beth Bilderback
Jim Bryant	Greg Coco
James Clouse	Louise Arnold-Friend
Janice Frye	Robert Gale
A. Wilson Greene	Randy Hackenburg
John Hennessy	Anne Harris
Robert K. Krick	JoAnna McDonald
Warren Motts	Brian Pohanka
Donald Pfanz	Frank O'Reilly
Richard Sommers	Mike Winey
Jack Wise	Mac Wycoff

TravelBrains Trivia Questions

Q1 ...... B
Q2 ...... A
Q3 C
Q4 ...... A

Photo Credits
Picture credits are listed by page number from left to right, top to bottom.

7: Library of Congress, MASS-MOLLUS/USAMHI, Carlisle, PA. 9: Gettysburg NMP, MASS-MOLLUS/USAMHI. 10: Fredericksburg & Spotsylvania NMP, Library of Congress 11: Dale Gallon Historical Art, Gettysburg, PA, Fredericksburg & Spotsylvania NMP, Fredericksburg, VA. 12: National Archives, Library of Congress. 14: The Museum of the Confederacy, Richmond, VA. 16: MASS-MOLLUS/USAMHI, Surgeon's saw, Motts Military Museum. 17: Pennsylvania Capital Preservation Committee, Harrisburg, PA, MASS-MOLLUS/USAMHI, Officer's Sword carried By Colonel Zin - Gregory A. Coco Collection, Gettysburg, PA, *Confederate Veteran Magazine* Volume 7 (1899). 18,19: Anne S.K. Brown Military Collection, Brown University, Providence. 21: MASS-MOLLUS/USAMHI, Gettysburg NMP, Gettysburg, PA. 22,23: National Archives, Fredericksburg & Spotsylvania NMP. 25: MASS-MOLLUS/USAMHI, Library of Congress. 26,27: *Battles and Leaders* Vol. 3. 28: Hunter, *Confederate Veteran Magazine* Vol. 13 (1905), South Caroliniana Library, University of South Carolina, MASS-MOLLUS/USAMHI. 29: *Battles and Leaders* Vol. 3, MASS-MOLLUS/USAMHI. 30: MASS-MOLLUS/USAMHI, Powell 24th NC, *Clark's North Carolina Regiments* Vol. 2. 31:MASS-MOLLUS/USAMHI, Valentine Museum/Richmond History Center, Richmond, VA. 34: National Archives, Frank & Marie-Therese Wood Print Collections, Alexandria, VA. 35:Fredericksburg & Spotsylvania NMP, Burnside Carbine, Fields Of Glory, Gettysburg, PA. 36: MASS-MOLLUS/USAMHI. 37: MASS-MOLLUS/USAMHI. 38: *Battles and Leaders* Vol. 3.

Music Credits
Megatrax Music Library
Brent Smith using samples from the Ilio Music Library

Voice Credits
In order of appearance

Narrator	Reg Green
Tour Guide	Debby Winsberg
Union Engineer & Soldier of the 34th NY	Jim Davis
Josiah Favill, Pvt. William Kepler & Gen. Darius Couch	Terence Rae
Fredericksburg civilian & poetry	Carrie Gordon Lowrey
Benjamin Borton & Pvt. Erskine Church	Patrick Seitz
Col. Henry Zinn	Carl Jaecke
William Owen	P. M. Howard
Gen. Thomas Meagher	Bob Loza
Col. Edward Cross & Col. Samuel Zook	Bill von Ravensberg
Pvt. Alexander Hunter & Confederate soldier	Gary Sturm
Brig. Gen. Joseph Kershaw	Michael Robinson
Lt. Charles Powell	Lance Arthur Smith
Edward Heinichen	Stan Sorensen

Special thanks to the Janitor, Mom, Thea, Jennie, and the VA legal eagles.

©2001 TravelBrains, Inc.
Fredericksburg Battlefield Guidebook
TravelBrains Fredericksburg Team: Michael S. Conaway, Catherine R. Davis, Paul C. Davis, Victor J. Davis, Ryan P. Gould and Wayne E. Motts.

Fredericksburg Field Guide, Fredericksburg Expedition Guide and Fredericksburg Animated are trademarks of TravelBrains, Inc. All Rights Reserved. No portion of this book may be reproduced in any form or by any means without explicit written permission from TravelBrains, Inc.